CRANACH

CRANACH

BY

PIERRE DESCARGUES

HARRY N. ABRAMS, INC. · PUBLISHERS
NEW YORK

LIBRARY OF CONGRESS CATALOG CARD NUMBER: 61-11936
TRANSLATED FROM THE FRENCH BY HELEN RAMSBOTHAM
PUBLISHED IN THE UNITED STATES OF AMERICA, 1961
ALL RIGHTS RESERVED

45415

LUCAS CRANACH THE ELDER

Most art historians will claim that the golden age of German painting, which cast its glow over two centuries, was rich in great painters, among whom were two geniuses : Dürer and Grünewald. They claim two and not three geniuses, for they exclude Lucas Cranach the Elder. They allow him to have been a good painter, and their books reproduce his pictures rather than those of Burgkmair, Altdorfer or Baldung Grien ; but they are reserved in their judgment of Cranach's career, even going so far as to accuse him of mass production.

For the glorification of his patrons, the Electors of Saxony, Lucas Cranach did indeed paint portraits of Frederick the Wise and John the Faithful sixty times each during one year. He can be accused of wasting himself on hack work, and on engravings for the title pages of books in which he did not even try to develop his own particular talents, since he merely contented himself with carrying out the task adequately. Finally, his manner of stressing the erotic in his paintings of nudes might be attributed to his business sense rather than to an obsession.

Cranach neither lived nor worked like a genius, in the contemporary sense of a genius—striding "mighty and alone" at the head of his people and of the world of art. Genius never repeats itself, never demeans itself by hack work, and never scatters its powers indiscriminately. It concentrates all its energies into the painting of a few great pictures.

Grünewald's name suggests the *Crucifixion* of the Isenheim Altarpiece, Dürer's suggests *Melencolia* or *Knight, Death, and Devil;* but when the name of Cranach is mentioned, a series of lightly clad, graceful maidens comes to mind, no one

Venus being greater than another. Cranach's name evokes not so much a single masterpiece as a *school* of painting. To discredit him, it might be added that on several occasions Cranach deliberately ignored the most *avant-garde* elements of his time.

He was a reactionary, then, who was not a genius. Melanchthon, with Aristotelean logic, finds the right place for him: he draws up a hierarchy chosen from the most important German painters of the 15th and 16th centuries, with Dürer representing *genius grande,* Grünewald *genius mediocre,* and Cranach *genius humile* (a fine talent but not great). These distinctions may seem academic to us today, yet when properly stressed they are still valid, for the chief accusation brought against Cranach is not that he painted badly but that he painted too much, that he lived at an ordinary level, not on the mysterious heights of the great masters, and did not keep his distance from us as they do. He was a materially minded man who did not see why painting should not be put to commercial use, reproduced and copied several times if necessary, and in his need he worked as much for others as for himself. He was not the only artist to do so, but in his case it stands out. Less independent than Dürer and more fortunate than the unlucky Grünewald, Cranach achieved social success. Germany was far less flamboyant than Italy, yet he was Court painter to the Electors of Saxony, just as Mantegna was to the Dukes of Mantua, with all the duties, tedium, and rewards that such an appointment entailed. This may have obliged him to take up a prudent attitude toward *avant-garde* aesthetic ideas, but on the other hand he was able to sign pictures with his arms—a winged serpent—for he was ennobled, whereas Dürer signed with his initials alone (though not without pride): the only official mark of favor he received was a pension from the Emperor. Melanchthon shows great perspicacity therefore in attributing Cranach's painting, so popular in his own day, to his *genius humile.*

What kind of a man was this *genius humile?* Self-portraits were rare at that time and although Dürer painted himself readily at all ages in his most handsome clothes Cranach's only likenesses of himself are to be found in various disguises among the crowds peopling some of his canvases. There is just one self-portrait, however, in the Uffizi Gallery at Florence, an austere picture of a noble old man, who reappears at Weimar in the Stadtkirche Altarpiece, standing with clasped hands at the foot of the Cross while the blood of the Redeemer falls in baptism upon his head. The superscription of the Uffizi portrait says : *Aetatis suae 77.* He is soberly dressed, with thick white hair, his mouth hidden by an enormous mustache and a long bifurcated beard. The eyes are searching and compelling, the expression full of authority. The Master of *genius humile* sees himself as a leader—the father of a family, the head of a studio, engaged in intellectual fighting for the Reformation—fighting to such purpose, moreover, that he was at that time exiled from his own town of Wittenberg : this may explain the element of sadness or anxiety in his expression. The old man revealed to us here is very different from the painter of smiling nudes. He is far more like the artist who tried to revive religious iconography and to found a school of "Protestant Painting," or the tragic and violent young artist who painted the Crucifixions: for there were several Cranachs. Yet he was always an honest man whose own life reflected the upheavals of his day.

We know that Lucas Cranach's real name was Lucas Sunder or Lucas Maler and that he was called Cranach after his native town of Kronach (in Franconia, north of Bavaria, not far from Coburg, Bayreuth, and Bamberg). A very common name, Maler or Mahler, that is, painter, so he was known by the name of his town. This provided an opportunity for a play on words, then very popular, with the Greek *chronos* (time).

We know from the date of his birth (October 4, 1472) that he was a year younger than Dürer, a year older than Burgkmair, three years older than Grünewald, eight years older than Altdorfer, Jörg Breu, and Ratgeb, 18 years older than Wolf Huber, and 25 years older than Hans Holbein the Younger. Compared with the Dutch and Flemish painters he was six years younger than Massys, the contemporary of Gossaert and Mostaert, of Patinir (who died in 1524), of Gerard David (his senior by twelve years), and of Geertgen tot Sint Jans (his senior by seven years). Compared with the Italians, he was 41 years younger than Mantegna and Giovanni Bellini, 37 years younger than Cosimo Tura, 27 years younger than Botticelli, and 20 years younger than Leonardo, but he was three years older than Michelangelo and 11 years older than Raphael.

We must not deduce from his nearness in time to Michelangelo that Cranach was motivated by the same aesthetic curiosity. Although battle was well and truly joined between the new Italian style of painting and the established school of the Dutch and Flemish painters, with Van der Weyden and Memling at its head and Quentin Massys and Geertgen tot Sint Jans as its crowning glory, the German painters stood apart, making their pilgrimages at times to Venice, at times to Bruges, returning home to face problems of quite another kind, which had less to do with aesthetics than with traits of national character. For Germany was out of tune. She saw the Germanic Holy Roman Empire crumbling and Rome escaping her. The attractions of Italy might glitter more brightly than ever, but the German States remained impervious; they were driven in upon themselves, in the throes of a crisis which led to social revolution of a kind hitherto unknown in Europe and to the foundation of a new religion. There was of course no real innovation here, but the expression of long-standing grievances; yet from this return to the sources and from self-communion came original inspiration and spiritual enrichment.

The persistence of Gothic art in Germany was not a sign of devotion to past glories, as in the Low Countries; it took on the character of a new enterprise with all its attendant risks. This is particularly so in Cranach's case.

THE CRUCIFIXION. c. 1500
KUNSTHISTORISCHES MUSEUM, VIENNA

Whereas first Dürer and then Holbein became the champions of international art, Cranach after some preliminary hesitation chose to stay firmly on German ground. Unlike Grünewald who staked his all on mediaeval thought, breathing new life into it with a force we are only just beginning to recognize, Cranach was to be attracted first by one extreme and then by the other. He was familiar with Dürer, the master who had been converted to the new ways. He succeeded Jacopo de' Barbari, the Italian theorist, as Court painter at Wittenberg, but the marvels of perspective seemed to him merely triumphs of virtuosity. He tried his hand at this and then went back to the kind of painting that appealed to men nurtured and at home in the mediaeval tradition. The earliest pictures that can definitely be attributed to him date from the beginning of the 16th century, which means that little or nothing is known of the first thirty years of his life. He probably lived at Kronach until 1500 or thereabouts, when it is likely that he went first to Coburg, then to Vienna, where he spent four or five years.

Cranach chose Vienna because Maximilian's city was at that time full of new ideas and in the throes of intellectual growth. The University (second in seniority to Prague among German-speaking universities) attracted a number of wandering scholars of all nationalities, who all spoke the same language, Latin, and who went on to teach either in London or in Rome, in Nürnberg or Amsterdam. Among the great teachers then were Conrad Celtes and Johannes Cuspinian, the chief exponents of humanism of their day. Celtes taught rhetoric and poetry and was universally acclaimed as a perfect reincarnation of a classic poet. He wrote Latin epigrams and odes, and the title of his most important poem has an Ovidian flourish: the *Quatuor Libri Amorum*. Burgkmair, the most Italianate of the Augsburg artists, painted Celtes' portrait, and in an engraving, dated 1501, Dürer drew a picture of him presenting his works to the Emperor Maximilian and to Frederick the Wise, Elector of Saxony. Dürer also made a frontispiece for the *Libri*

10

Amorum in 1502, which amounts to a manifesto in favor of classicism—indeed, it is more of an advertisement than a frontispiece, bringing in the Chaldaeans, the Egyptians, Plato, Vergil, and Cicero : Celtes is the standard-bearer of humanism. Cuspinian himself had the reputation of a prodigy. He received the title of Rector Magnificus of the University by the Emperor's favor when he was only 27. He recited the glories of the Caesars to Maximilian, who asked nothing better than to follow their example, dreaming of Roman triumphs to such an extent that he had an engraving made by Dürer of a Roman triumph of his own. Thus Vienna at the beginning of the 16th century was almost more Roman than in the days when the Legions called it Vindobona or when Marcus Aurelius died there. Southern Germany as a whole was seized with a passion for classicism. At Augsburg, the Fugger banking family were entertaining Latinist artists and scholars. At Nürnberg, one Pirckheimer was collecting classical antiques and defending Dürer as leader of the *avant-garde*. At Basel, new books illustrated by new artists were being published. These cities are all at the gates of Italy, but Germany was not inspired by what was happening at the beginning of the century in Venice, where Giorgione and Titian were breaking new ground. Germany's interest in the classics was serious, whereas Giorgione's treatment of his ruins was already becoming playful, almost romantic. Germany venerated Andrea Mantegna as the greatest artist of the century and with him Pollaiuolo and Tura, among others. Italian art was known to foreigners through engravings : prints were circulated among those who could not travel beyond the Alps, just as Dürer was known in Italy through his engravings and the copies by Marcantonio Raimondi. Dürer himself copied the *Battle of Sea Gods* painted by Mantegna. The master of Mantua was admired not only for his talent but also for the frescoes he painted—those " classic " frescoes among which can be found centurions' armor, bas-reliefs, medallions, a whole classic past which he reproduced faithfully with an archaeologist's attention to detail.

This art of toga and battle array, where Christianity adopted pagan allegories and Catholicism joined forces with classic philosophy, made up the intellectual climate of the *avant-garde* in Germany.

EARLY DAYS

Lucas Cranach was certainly not in tune with his times, judging from the first picture attributed to him, a *Crucifixion* in the Museum at Vienna. It is a picture full of violence, in the true Gothic tradition, showing the place of execution. A dog is gnawing at decaying arms; the foreground is heaped with spines and skulls to which still cling a few handfuls of hairs. Hanging on the three crosses, Christ and the two thieves appear as bleeding flesh twisted in agony against a blue sky banked with clouds. On the ground some ghoulish characters looking ridiculous in Oriental dress, mounted on horses whose legs are overlapped, are gazing at the wounded Christ; the sponge soaked in vinegar is being offered to Him, while the Blessed Virgin faints. It is exactly the kind of picture in which the artist avoids difficulties: there is little movement, the construction and grouping of the figures is mediocre, and the composition is awkward. It is obvious that Cranach, then aged 28, had not been painting for long; and yet this *Crucifixion* has proved to be one of the most moving pictures of its time and one of those nearest to us in feeling.

What kind of painting had Cranach seen in Bavaria and Austria that made him refuse rather than welcome any new ideas? There, Gothic art still lingered, in two forms. In the hands of Rueland Frueauf the Younger, the Master of Mondsee, and the Master of Grossgmain it reached extremes of precision and of formal perfection; yet in actual fact these painters of the late 15th and early 16th centuries (in the Klosterneuburg altarpiece, for instance) were only perfecting the supremely elegant style achieved by the Master of the Upper Rhine nearly a century

14   PORTRAIT OF DR. JOHANNES CUSPINIAN. c. 1502
OSKAR REINHART COLLECTION, WINTERTHUR

PORTRAIT OF ANNA CUSPINIAN. c. 1502   15
OSKAR REINHART COLLECTION, WINTERTHUR

earlier, in 1410, when he painted the *Virgin and Child in the Garden of Paradise.*

The other form of Late Gothic art derived from Hans Multscher's grinning faces or from Hans Hirtz's caricatures. Maleskircher's expressionism, as shown in his Nürnberg *Crucifixion,* was ahead of his time. This expressionism can be seen as well in Jan Polak's roughhewn figures in Munich : they are full of horror and violence and of appalling details, piled one upon the other to their common detriment. Grüne- wald alone knew how to make horror great.

Dürer was alone therefore in his search for a new style of painting. History cuts to the quick : it is the geometricians among the late 15th century painters who are chiefly remembered today, for their initiative in looking at the world in a revolutionary way. There can be no doubt that their pictures represent a turning point in human thought, yet they were not the only painters who took part in the revolution. Others were taking other risks at the very same time, unobtrusively, with no publicity and no parade of key names or theories : theirs was a revolution in landscape painting.

Historians all speak of a mysterious and vague Danube school of painting, but they cannot bring proof of this, for there were no theorists behind it to formulate a common declaration of faith. It was a revolution of solitaries—indeed, it can be said that it was a perfect example of the intro- version which, as has already been seen, characterized Ger- many at that time. On the one hand the revolutionaries set themselves against abstract construction and would have nothing to do with morphological analysis of creatures and things, on the other hand they plunged into the study of nature—the one subject which can be thoroughly mastered without scientific technique.

Cranach's connection with the Danube school remains hypothetical; it seems likely that landscape painting only became fashionable there after he had gone to Wittenberg to work for the Elector of Saxony. If he was connected with it, this can be traced only in the landscapes which he uses

16

as backgrounds to his portraits or as part of his compositions. There is in fact a striking connection between Cranach's painting of the Crucifixion among trees on the banks of a river, which could be the Danube, and similar landscapes by Altdorfer or Wolf Huber. A resemblance can also be traced between the background landscapes of the portraits of Johannes Cuspinian and Stefan Reuss and those masses of leafy branches behind Altdorfer's triumphant St. George. There has been an attempt to deduce from the meticulous treatment of nature by all these painters that they were following Cranach, because he was older than the masters of the Danube school.

In fact he was simply giving proof, a little ahead of them, of the interest in urban and rural landscape painting latent at that time in Southern Germany and Austria. The perspective of Michael Pacher's streets, Marx Rurchlich's city squares, the elegant lines of Rueland Frueauf's landscapes, and the wealth of manuscript illustrations were preparing the way for Dürer's amazing landscapes, which he was to carry out in watercolor or in line engraving in the neighborhood of Nürnberg and on his journeys to the Low Countries and to Venice, and for Albrecht Altdorfer's *Battle of Arbeles,* which is the supreme example of that school of painting. Cranach's landscapes, however, take on a definite character and are marked by an original quality—ambiguity. This can be seen as much in the backgrounds of the portraits of Johannes Cuspinian and his wife (1502) as in the wild scenery of an engraving of 1509 (much influenced by Dürer) showing the penance of St. John Chrysostom. Trees and stones, rivers and rocks, roots and castles, leaves and clouds are obvious, but on close investigation the mountains seem to disguise some face, the tree trunks some animal, while some creature's eye leers from the ground. In these pictures nature appears to be in a permanent state of gestation. Animal, vegetable, and mineral are no longer perfectly distinct. A tuft of grass may be a bird of paradise, a cloud a face, and the lines of a pine branch may also be those of a prophet's or an Elector's beard.

Each detail of the landscape has a counterpart in another kingdom, and is thus bound up with all the elements. There is deliberate "animation" here.

Jerome Bosch and Bruegel carry "animation" so far as to give definite shape to their monsters : the stones have claws, the trees have eyes. The metamorphosis is complete, whereas with Cranach it remains potential. The symbolical owl and parrot, astrological emblems of Johannes and Anna, the stars shining in full daylight, and the fires lighting up the sky in the portraits of the two Cuspinians, like the summer and winter trees giving time and season to those of Stefan Reuss and his wife, are simply natural phenomena brought to light. Elsewhere they are waiting to be exposed and interpreted. We can feel them close at hand, as if nature is on the point of giving birth. There is nothing scientific about this knowledge, which here reaches its heights ; a century later it will have been forgotten, and today we find it very difficult to decipher Jerome Bosch's or Cranach's symbols.

Cranach himself is characteristic of the typical retreat to German positions and of the German refusal to accept the Italian revolution ; he played a definite part in this supreme late flowering of the Middle Ages, whose beauty was thrown into relief, although despised and left behind, by the new ideas of the Renaissance. This system of self-defense bore fruit. It is usual to speak of the spell cast over Germany by Venice, Milan, or Florence, but mention should also be made of the influence of Germany on Italy and the Low Countries. To quote Vasari : "Every cobbler's booth has its German landscape," and there are indisputable signs of German influence in some of Giorgione's and Lotto's landscapes and in the pictures of Patinir, Met de Bles, Lucas van Leyden, and later of Roelant Savery, who traveled in the Tirol. Yet for all its considerable influence, and however moving the picture of nature which it drew, German art has no historical importance because it played no part in the revolution brought about by the Renaissance painters : by missing this boat it missed a place in history.

THE PARENTS OF CHRIST. 1509
STAEDEL INSTITUTE, FRANKFURT

THE HOLY FAMILY. 1509   21
STAEDEL INSTITUTE, FRANKFURT

We can now see Cranach in relation to the prevailing ideas of his time. In the Kunsthistorisches Museum at Vienna there is a *St. Jerome* depicting the hermit with his lion, not far from a town but in wild country in the midst of trees and rocks, where dead and living branches intermingle: he is tearing his beard and chastising himself with a stone, dedicating his sufferings to the bleeding Christ who looks down on him from the Cross. An owl, watched over by a parrot (symbols once again), is gazing at the scene with round eyes glowing among the dark leaves. This picture was painted in 1502, and is the work of an accomplished artist who is no longer avoiding the difficulties, as he did in the preceding *Crucifixion*. It has the quality of a masterpiece. From 1502 until 1504, indeed, Cranach painted a series of pictures which place him among the chief artists of his day. These are the *Crucifixion* of 1503 (Munich), the portraits of the Cuspinians of 1502 (Winterthur) and of the Reuss family (Nürnberg and Berlin) of 1503 (one is dated 1502), a *Christ in the Garden of Olives*, and a picture of St. Stephen. They are confused, perhaps, but this must be accepted, for they were never intended to be orderly. It is sometimes difficult to make out the fantastic features, the swarms of gestures, objects, and faces jostling each other in this twisted world where noses and breastplates, the blood of men, and the sap of trees, fingers, and blades of grass are of equal value. The crucified figures hang broken on their crosses, lost in horror, while the crowd below tramples on dismembered corpses. There is no accident about this confusion: it is the work of an expert who knows how to throw Christ's agony and prayer into relief above a fearful dark abyss where an angel of mercy lies hidden.

Cranach was a master of engraving as well as of painting. At thirty he was at the height of his powers, uniting and surpassing in his talent the two main features of Late Gothic art: the subtlety of landscape glimpsed through the subject matter, and the tragic violence of the Passion behind the obvious.

PORTRAIT OF A YOUNG GIRL. c. 1520
THE LOUVRE, PARIS ▷

Cuspinian in his portrait is full of vitality, even of fervor. The young Rector Magnificus of the University of Vienna, bull-like in his red hat and rich fur coat, is grasping a closed book with passionate determination, as if fighting for truth and freedom against the ambiguous world of day and night, good and evil, with which Cranach has surrounded him. Reuss has his hands planted on the open pages of a book as if clinging to the only thing in which he can believe. There is nothing conventional in the pictures of these men who championed the liberty of the 16th-century *avant-garde*, for the reason that reading was then an act of faith; but Cranach might simply have shown them in the time-honored manner in which the prophets are pictured with Alpha and Omega in holy books, whereas truth itself is here in new and shining colors, eternally alive.

In the Munich Pinakothek *Crucifixion,* a wind-tossed storm overshadows the three dark crucified figures and the landscape of river and mountain stretching away beneath Christ on his Cross; enshrouded in the trees are the two thieves, the first just visible in profile, the second half hidden by the first; the Blessed Virgin gazes upward, keeping her eyes fixed on Christ and ignoring them, like St. John, who shares her grief. A great deal has been written about this picture— about the landscape to begin with, as proving that Lucas Cranach belonged to the Danube school, and then about St. John's very stature : he has the same slender proportions here as Grünewald gives him in the panel of the Isenheim altarpiece, where he holds the Mater Dolorosa in his arms. Finally the hands and their odd mannerisms come under discussion—those hands joined by the Blessed Virgin and St. John in complicated elegant gestures, arms linked, fingers forming two flowers, just as they appear also in the Colmar Museum picture : hands of communion, hands of sorrow, dead hands and living hands, hands of martyrs and of those who rejoice ... As for the Danube School, we have already seen that there is no real proof that Cranach was connected with the painters of Venice and Ratisbon ; but it is another question where Grünewald is concerned. We know that he worked at Aschaffenburg in Franconia, that Cardinal Albrecht of Brandenburg was his patron as well as Cranach's, and that he died in Halle, a Saxon town like Wittenberg and Weimar. If Grünewald really was born in 1455, which would make him seventeen years older than Cranach, his genius flowered very late; for the Isenheim masterpiece is supposed to have been painted between 1510 and 1516, whereas the *Crucifixion* by Cranach under discussion was painted in 1503, and it is unlikely that so unique and unchanging a painter as Grünewald was influenced by the variable Cranach. What can be the explanation? Let us simply accept Cranach's brilliant debut for what it was. He is loved, and will always be loved, for a mere handful of his pictures. It can truly be said that the first Cranach died in 1503 and that he did nothing better afterward. At 31 he gave up tragic art, the work of a mediaeval painter who calmly fused classic mythology with his own vision in order to show the absurdity of the former, as in the engraving he made in 1503 for the Passau Missal, where aging Cupids are ranged above the whole monstrous menagerie of the Middle Ages. In this picture he runs the gamut of horror, from its misshapen depths to its grotesque heights. A child with wizened face and protruding stomach is playing the flute; a garland surrounds the whole, framing St. Stephen who carries the embers which have burned him and will burn him forever, his head crowned by a halo of vine branches, his face that of a brute suddenly and miraculously transformed by gentleness. It is as if the painter were showing us that the Italian style merely gilds the lily.

A NEW STYLE OF PAINTING

Cranach's second phase was to last for nearly half a century, during which he entered fresh fields, oblivious of his first few masterpieces. When he was about fifty years old, Dürer was to see him and depict him as a man full of care, with

luxuriant hair, mustache, and beard, a ferocious look in one eye, the other expressing all the doubt in the world. What we know of Cranach does indeed seem to tally with the version shown us by the greatest artist of his day : he was sorely tried by his experiences, and he is all the more appealing in that he was as closely in touch with the important happenings of his time and suffered as much from its conflicts as we suffer from those of our day. He knew what it was to go into hiding and exile ; he painted sometimes for the joy of expressing himself and sometimes as a duty for the edification of mankind, just like those tortured artists and poets of our own day whose hopes and sorrows are familiar to us. No doubt there are geniuses who can be understood outside their own epoch, such as Albrecht Dürer, Cranach's contemporary, with all his aesthetic and personal complexities. But this is not true of Cranach. Anyone who takes the trouble to study his period and look closely at his work will see that Cranach was truly time-bound.

In 1504, Cranach gave up tragic painting and adopted

DETAIL OF VIRGIN AND CHILD

VIRGIN AND CHILD. c. 1518
GEMÄLDEGALERIE, KARLSRUHE

27

quite a different style in his *Rest on the Flight into Egypt* (Berlin Museum). It has been snowing in his Egypt and there are pine trees, cedars, and birches. Angels and cherubs, who are charming here, neither too demure nor too austere, swarm round Joseph and the Virgin and Child in a picturesque group. One holds a bird, another fetches water from a nearby stream, another plays the flute, and a fourth offers fruit and leaves to the Child. These angels and cherubs prove that Cranach has succumbed to the Italian style, but its influence is mitigated by the strength of the admirable German setting : look at the pine tree soaring up out of the picture against a clear cold blue sky, probably at the beginning of spring, since there are still patches of snow on the branches. Cranach has allowed himself the luxury of a beautiful study of draperies : the Flemish scarlet of Mary's dress falls in a thousand folds, far more than necessary, on to the flowery Ronsardian greensward at her feet.

This picture is important because it is a microcosm of Cranach's future style. It is drawn in rounded lines : the shape matters here more than the play of light and shade, for it is the work of a draughtsman who uses color merely as a decoration, albeit he does so with exquisite skill. Everything is typical. The man Cranach paints is surely the one he sees in his mirror, with hollow eyes, high cheekbones and long-lobed ears ; the solemn, simple way in which he holds his hat is copied from the gesture of his own left hand, seen in the mirror, where it becomes the right, while his own right hand, the one that draws and paints, cheats and pretends here to lean on a stick. Cranach was only 32 at this time, but he must have made himself look older in this picture. Later on, as a spirited Adam beside a charming Eve, he made himself look younger. It might be supposed that the Virgin of this *Rest on the Flight into Egypt* would be the new Madame Cranach, née Barbara Brengbier, the burgomaster's daughter whom he had just married at Gotha, but she is reputed to have been not at all pretty. Some other explanation must be found, therefore, for the beauty he so often painted, nude or clothed, in pagan or Christian religious context, and the most likely is that by 1504 he had formulated his own "typical man" and "typical woman." At any rate there is no connection between these small rounded figures with their delicate joints (like those of Bouts) and the Virgin and St. John of the preceding year's *Crucifixion,* nor is there any connection between the lines of this new picture and those of the *Crucifixion,* which form groups of unfurled sails—sails of stormy clouds, sails falling in weird bunches from Christ's girdle, draped fantastically around St. John and spreading across the sand where the river's course flows light and dark. All this has gone, and a far more varied interplay of shapes has taken its place.

A great deal must have happened between 1503 and 1504 to transform the painter of the heavy figures in the Munich *Crucifixion* into the elegant artist of the Berlin *Flight.* It is certainly true that 1504 was the year in which Frederick the Wise, Elector of Saxony, took Cranach into his service, but it was not this appointment which effected the sudden transformation. A far more important development has taken place. The appearance of the cherubs, smiling now whereas last year he was painting them with scorn, is probably due to his wish to be up to date and, setting aside historical logic, the little angel playing the flute in the foreground has obviously escaped from some Roman painting; but all this does not matter. The picture convinces us that something more than a formal conversion has taken place. In so far as we can be certain that the earlier pictures and engravings were all painted by the same hand, 1504 must be considered as a crucial year in Cranach's career, like the year in which Watteau discovered himself through Rubens, or the year when Picasso found himself by way of Lautrec. The trouble is that we do not know who Cranach was before he discovered himself. Maleskircher? Or pseudo-Maleskircher? Or the providential Mathis Neithardt Gothardt called Grünewald, whose probable date of birth ranges over some twenty years and who is supposed to have made countless journeys from one end of

Germany to the other (which is not unlikely). However this may be, there is a great deal to be said for the indecision and conflicting influences of the time : they fostered the young painter's own period of hesitancy and exploration and gave rise to a series of violent pictures, which are the work of a genius.

To simplify things we can say that a second life began for Cranach when he entered the service of Frederick the Wise. We know that Frederick had a great interest in painting, not unmixed with snobbishness, as, for instance, when he sought out Jacopo de' Barbari, the Italian painter and theorist of the new school, and appointed him to his Court at Wittenberg. He was also interested in relics, and is said to have owned thousands of fragments of crosses, heads of nails, strips of linen, pieces of bone and of heart, and faded eyes, all these holy remains being housed in appropriate reliquaries. Following the example of the Dukes of Mantua, who had their castle decorated with paintings by Mantegna, the first commission Frederick gave Cranach was to decorate his own castle with frescoes. Nothing remains of these frescoes today. A woodcut made by Cranach at this period bears for the first time the two blazoned escutcheons of the Electors of Saxony. St. Roch, St. Stephen, St. John, and the Virgin kneel in front of the most German of landscapes and a castle (which may be Frederick's) with a profusion of towers ; above them, in an escutcheon showing a heart stained with drops from the Grail, hangs a Christ with grief-distorted features, raised by the triple arms of the Cross, of his arms and of the draperies which flutter curiously around him.

In this picture the figures still have the tragic grandeur of those in the Munich *Crucifixion,* yet Cranach has become a Court painter. We may wonder, therefore, whether he was appointed because of the Munich *Crucifixion* or because of the *Rest on the Flight into Egypt.*

German painting cannot easily be separated from religious teaching. Engraving was far more in touch with daily life and gives us an excellent idea of what Germany was like at that

THE VIRGIN UNDER THE APPLE TREE. c. 1515–20
HESSISCHES LANDESMUSEUM, DARMSTADT

time, but painting was only detached from religion with great difficulty. It was largely through Cranach, and later through Baldung Grien and the *Landsknecht* painters in Switzerland, that painting was freed from its religious associations and brought on to the plane of cultured pleasure. Cranach was to paint pictures of nymphs, of Venus, Omphale, Lucretia, and Cupid, and of goddesses vying with each other before Paris—in other words, a series of attractive nudes in a setting that had nothing to do with religion, and Cranach did this so successfully that the elegance and lightness of touch which he used in these pictures became part of his whole technique. It can be seen in the portraits of the Madonna and in the illustrations to Protestant teaching which Cranach was to carry out later on, when Court painting ceased to be frivolous and took on a moralistic function, when the fashion for classic and Italian styles gave way to Protestantism, and serious pictures with such themes as " Suffer little children to come unto me " took the place of Venus. Court painting, as we understand it, did not last long in Germany. It is significant that Cranach the Tragic should represent this frivolous interlude in the history of a country which was to make a deliberate pursuit of seriousness.

A MASTERPIECE

Cranach's debut at Frederick's Court was not that of a frivolous artist, however, as that first woodcut shows. His first painting was an altarpiece for the Church in Wittenberg Castle (this picture was destroyed in 1760). He next painted the *Martyrdom of St. Catherine,* one of the most beautiful pictures of the century, now in the Dresden Museum. It is a triptych, with a large central panel, and two side panels each showing three saints : Barbara, Ursula, and Margaret on one side, Dorothy, Agnes, and Cunegunda on the other. The large central panel ($47^1/4 \times 39^3/16$ inches) shows an extraordinary concentration of events and allusions, producing a brilliant and mysterious effect.

32

Catherine in her finest dress, its gold-embroidered folds rippling over the grass, kneels with clasped hands in front of the wheel on which she is to be broken, while the central figure of the picture, a huge, long-legged executioner painted in many colors and elegant in slashed doublet and knots of ribbon, draws his sword. Meanwhile Augustus Maxentius tumbles off his horse, appalled at the lightning crashing from Heaven and setting fire to the wheel of execution.

So much for the main subject matter of the picture and for its principal story; but Cranach does not limit himself to these three characters. On the left he brings in Frederick the Wise and John the Faithful on horseback, preceded by a white-plumed squire bearing a lance. Rising above his patrons, who thus make their abrupt entry into the legend of St. Catherine, he depicts a mighty fortress. Historians are not certain whether it is meant to represent that of Torgau or of Coburg (the picture was probably painted for the Church at Torgau). Beneath the castle a river with houses on its banks flows through wooded country. The three spectators behold more than an outburst of divine wrath : extraordinary things are happening, for on the right, between Catherine and the flaming wheel, Cranach has arranged a curious cascade of seven heads balanced uncertainly upon each other, with arms and legs into the bargain, so that an assistant executioner standing just above the flames flings up his arms to Heaven in distraction. It all seems very confused, yet the artist has brought order into the picture in various ways.

First of all it is very well lighted. Catherine's face radiates brightness in front of the gray mass of the tottering heads, which are lit up in their turn by the burning wheel. There are living heads and dead heads, heads fantastically lighted from above or below according to their position in the vortex that engulfs them. Augustus Maxentius and the executioner, for their part, are struck with deadly pallor by the light from the sky. Finally the patrons on horseback, drawn and agitated, are seen in quite a different light. With admirable subtlety this painting groups its characters on different planes of action

by means of the lighting. Cranach certainly had need of subtlety here, for never can there have been such an intricate composition. Apart from the central action, the meaning is conveyed by allusions, both through horses and through human bodies. The picture is so complicated that once we have grasped its main structure we may well wonder whether the whole of it is here, and also whether the painter has not simply crowded into it as many faces as he could. It is really a strange mixture of horses and heads, hands and legs, jumbled together in the glare of the fire in front of the one calm element in the picture—the landscape—as calm as the noble executioner with his Roman nose. There is another kind of order in the chaos let loose by the threatening clouds: it comes from the actors' expressions, isolating those untouched by fear—the three onlookers, the executioner, and the victim. We can see here a third way in which order is introduced, for they alone are impervious to the storm of divine wrath, remaining outside the zone of fire which marks the two spheres of action and sets the patrons themselves apart.

The obvious reason for such a confused picture from the hand of an artist whose compositions hitherto have been so brilliant, or at the very least perfectly clear, is that he is trying to say more than usual. It is a highly condensed summary: fifteen people, three horses, a castle, a landscape, and an executioner's wheel are all crowded on to this panel, which is less than forty inches wide. Look at the faces, especially those of the heads which are being dragged along in a tumbled heap to be crushed by the wheel in front of Catherine. It is hard not to see them as portraits. The man in the cap resembles Dr. Stefan Reuss; the face of the emaciated man suggests Melanchthon. Whom does the man poking his head between Catherine and the executioner resemble? Who was the model for the face with hair blown forward which is being crushed on the chest of the man already on fire? What can be the meaning of the resemblance between the noble old man with the white beard and Jerome Holzschuher? If this painting really depicts the martyrdom of the

36

fifty philosophers whom Catherine converted during an argument before Caesar, what contemporary philosophers had Cranach in mind, and what message did he mean to convey to them? The polemical nature of this picture must be recognized once we compare it with an engraving by Dürer on the same subject, dated 1497 or thereabouts: this simply depicts the spectators' horror and man's absurd helplessness in face of the wrath of God. Dürer stages the martyrdom of St. Catherine as a great drama, a foretaste of the Apocalypse, while Cranach draws us into a scene of fantastic intimacy. He dispenses theatrical effects, such as exaggerated facial expressions, to such an extent that the characters seem as impassive as models to whose features the painter has given no life, either because he wanted to be scrupulously accurate or because he lacked a sense of synthesis. However this may be, Cranach was a wonderful analyst and therefore an excellent portrait painter. His picture of St. Catherine is the first authoritative proof of this.

It also reveals his mastery of a new style. He was experimenting boldly, and the result is significant. The *Martyrdom* is the most sinuous of pictures, twisting and turning on a score of axes: Augustus and the man with his hands crossed on top of his head, the executioner's wheel, the falling heads on each side of the executioner, all revolve on different pivots. The horses and the elegant gait of the page add to the general swaying impression. It is as if an earthquake were taking place and the world convulsed by the fury of Heaven, yet on the face of it the picture is perfectly static.

Such is the first flowering of Cranach's new style. The six women surrounding the martyr on the two side panels are also painted with great suppleness, which here reaches elegance. The six saints, outdoing the Italians in their dazzlingly rich dresses with long folds and curved sleeves, bear witness that Cranach remained quite untouched by Jacopo de' Barbari's attempts to propagate the laws of perspective in Saxony, which lent so many complexities to Dürer's work. Cranach remained faithful to the sinuous Gothic line. We might

38   PORTRAIT OF A MAN. 1522
NATIONAL GALLERY OF ART, WASHINGTON, D. C. (KRESS COLLECTION)

PORTRAIT OF A WOMAN. 1522   39
NATIONAL GALLERY OF ART, WASHINGTON, D.C. (KRESS COLLECTION)

suppose that Cranach would have given up his Grünewaldian violence in order to follow the current aesthetic fashion; but it was not so. He was not tempted by the conquest of space but by a new realism, that of faces. No doubt what strikes us most, at first, in the two panels of saints is the magnificence of their dresses and the grace of their bearing; then we come to see that each one is highly original and a typical Cranach figure. We feel that we know Cunegunda and have often met Ursula . . . They are absolutely true to life, in spite of the archaic monster lying at their feet, caparisoned in scales as sumptuous as their dresses.

Cranach did not rebel against the mediaeval love of horrors, however. He managed to synchronize their unreality with his new-found reality. He even gave them flesh and blood and put new life into them, as we can see from the string of philosophers' heads dragged into the fire and the movement of the wheel on which Catherine is to be broken. In this same year—1506— he made a very fine engraving of the Temptation of St. Anthony, which resembles Dürer in technique and the *Temptation* of Grünewald's Isenheim altarpiece in its violence. The saint has been seized and lifted high into the air by hundreds and thousands of monsters, as high as the topmost branch of a tree (from which hang the inevitable arms of Saxony), above his hermit's cave; the grass grows like hairy paws, the tree trunks gape like mouths, and the dead branches are as threatening as claws. Here again the world has a double meaning. Grass, trees, and stones are not quite real: it is peopled by the whole of human thought and of animal creation. Anthony himself cannot easily be distinguished from his tormentors: the devil has taken almost complete possession of him. The Middle Ages lingered on thus in Cranach's work. Its unreality survived in another form in the composition depicting fourteen "intercessors" which he painted for the Church at Torgau in 1507. The artist has not bothered to explain the gestures or the arrangement of the crowd of saints, each brandishing his particular emblem— vanquished monsters, tamed beasts, or instruments of torture—

so that everyone can recognize his own patron. But he has taken great pains to show their difference in type: every age and stage of life is here, even if their expression of religious sentiment is unchanging.

What was Dürer painting at this period? The *Adoration of the Magi* (Uffizi), painted in 1504, is a masterpiece because of the ease and clarity with which he arranges his shapes, but the *Feast of the Rose Garlands* (Prague), painted in 1506, is a mass of faces. In the study, made in five days, of *Christ Among the Doctors* Dürer concentrates on facial expression in the style of Leonardo: he does not try to explain the grouping of the faces but gets his effect from their juxtaposition. Cranach's *Fourteen Intercessors* should probably be considered as a similar study. This shows that the new "expressionist" adventure could be as attractive for an artist at that time as "constructivism." While realizing the marvelous possibilities of perspective, Dürer is perfectly ready to bring his pictures to life by the juxtaposition of different faces. Cranach's *Martyrdom of St. Catherine* shows that he also could do this quite easily and naturally, without seeking violent contrasts, merely by emphasizing his subtle harmonies. It was not from ignorance that he held back from the international *avant-garde* and would only take part in the most moderate form of revolution. He thus affirmed his independence in a Court which vied with the Emperor for foreign theorists of advanced views. The picture of the *Fourteen Intercessors* is far from clear, though very striking, with its contrasts of armor, fustian, and embroidered cloth, of gentle faces and menacing monsters. No doubt it was impossible to fit everything into so small a canvas without giving an impression of jostling and confusion and, as we have seen, Cranach was similarly inspired in the picture of St. Catherine, though on a more spectacular scale. Apart from comparisons of quality, however, there is a definite hiatus between the engravings he made at that time, such as the *Temptation of St. Anthony* or that of the nude Magdalen carried up to Heaven by a flight of angels, and his paintings. There is a difference in tone which is really dis-

turbing. Each fresh example shows that Cranach used his engravings for storytelling and his paintings for human analysis.

Frederick required of him endless decorations (for the castle of Coburg especially), engravings, altarpieces, and designs for coins and medals. He must have been satisfied with his Court painter for on January 6, 1508, he ennobled him, giving him as his arms " *or* with a sable serpent, with bats' wings of the same, crowned with gules and holding in its mouth a ruby mounted on a gold ring." Was this two-winged serpent (beneficent also since it retrieved a lost jewel) a sign of Cranach's interest in science or simply a mark of distinction intended to facilitate the mission to the Emperor with which the Elector was entrusting him? Whatever the explanation, the artist signed his pictures with this winged serpent from 1509 onward, and it is thus of importance to historians. The tradition was that during the lifetime of the father, the son should modify the paternal signature slightly when making

ST. CHRISTOPHER. c. 1515
SCHLOSS ROHONCZ FOUNDATION,
LUGANO

use of the family arms on his own account. Some of the pictures leaving Cranach's studio from 1537 onward show the serpent with wings no longer perpendicular but horizontal. Lucas Cranach the Younger was then 22—a very good age to start painting—and this lowering of the wings may well indicate his signature. His elder brother, Hans, had died in Bologna that very year. This explanation of the variation in signature would enable us to distinguish between pictures so similar in style that it is difficult to tell which Cranach painted them.

THE JOURNEY TO THE LOW COUNTRIES

In 1508, at the end of the year, Cranach set off for the Low Countries to paint a portrait of Maximilian's grandson. The future Charles V was then eight years old. His proposed marriage to a princess of France, aged four, had been broken off owing to political fluctuations and Frederick was probably seeking a future ally by means of the picture (now lost) which his artist was to paint. If the honesty of the ruler of Saxony (exceptional among German Electors) were not so well known, it might be supposed that this approach was really intended as an appeal to poor Maximilian for a subsidy. But the pretext is not important: what matters is that Cranach thus got to know the Low Countries. He might have preferred to study Italian painting, like Dürer, who had just returned from Venice, but we cannot be certain of this. He was to spend several months dividing his time between Malines, Brussels, Antwerp, Ghent, and Bruges. What did he see there? We know that when Dürer in his turn reached the Low Countries he was impressed by the Van Eycks, the Van der Weydens, and the Van der Goes. Cranach left no chronicle of his travels, but the picture he painted on his return— an altarpiece of the Holy Family, now in the Staedel Institute at Frankfurt—is so different from his preceding work that we can easily see what new ideas Flanders gave him. Now indeed he takes account of space. Paved floors are

FONTIS NYMPHA SACRI SOMNVM
NE RVMPE QVIESCO

44   DIANA. c. 1530

MUSÉE DES BEAUX-ARTS, BESANÇON

45

shown in perfect perspective. There is fresh evidence of riches, not in the clothes this time but in the architecture : the round marble columns glitter, friezes of Cupids sculptured in bas-relief bear the arms of Saxony above the heads of the figures. The large windows of the Italianate palace open on to a Saxon countryside, still untamed, with its dark trees, somber forests, and menacing castles.

It is easy to see what inspired this new setting and whence blew the wind in whose air the figures move so much more freely. Yet in fact this Italian vision was really only a Flemish dream, for the pictures which Cranach saw in Antwerp were merely examples of the Italian style grafted on to the old Gothic root. The painters responsible for this, Quentin Massys, Jan Gossaert, and Adriaen Isenbrant, were his contemporaries. The Elector of Saxony's envoy must have been able to study Gossaert's work at the Hapsburg Court, at Malines or at Brussels, for Gossaert was Philip of Burgundy's Court painter : yet the earliest picture by Gossaert known to us is dated 1516—eight years too late. This is a painting of *Neptune and Amphitrite,* showing Dürer's influence ... Moreover Gossaert was traveling in Italy in 1508. Similarly there is more than one point of resemblance between Quentin Massys' *Holy Family* (Brussels Museum) and Cranach's Staedel Institute altarpiece. Yet this painting by Massys, if it is indeed the earliest known, is dated 1509 (one year too late). The connection is obvious, but cannot be proved. We must be content, therefore, with patent examples, merely noting that Cranach's visit to the Low Countries had a marked effect on him and that he assimilated a great deal from the *avant-garde* school of painting at Antwerp before its influence spread throughout the country. Owing to hasty transposition its Italian character was equivocal : Italian and Flemish idioms jostled each other in an undisciplined style, so that an abundant, redundant shape, an excess of outlandish decoration and a breadth of composition go hand in hand with clear, clean perfection and a rounded, finished, polished vision of the world.

46

Cranach assimilated new styles very rapidly : this was not the first time that he showed himself to be well ahead of the rest. From this point of view he may be considered one of those forerunners common to every age, quickly tiring of known pastures and eagerly opening the way to fresh fields. Did he not paint pictures foreshadowing the coming Altdorfer-Danube style, when he was in Austria at the beginning of his career ? And have we not just seen that his *Holy Family* could be taken for a rough sketch of Massys' famous picture ? We must be careful, however, not to accept hastily hypotheses about the 16th century. Cranach is the first artist to emerge from the shadows of the Middle Ages who gives us dates from which to take our bearings : we feel confident and so tend to forget that the ground is still being explored.

Cranach learned from the Low Countries lessons of clarity and space and how to bring columns and hangings into his décor ; but these did not really improve his style, merely adding heaviness to his composition and monotony to the interaction of his various groups of figures.

He was entering the most prolific period of his life, in which he reached an alarming rate of production. At 37 he was painting, illustrating, and decorating. Frederick ennobled him, exempted him from taxes, and made him present after present, but he was still in debt to his Court painter, for he exacted a great deal of work from him. The Elector, as we have seen, had a craze for collecting relics. He owned thousands—some say 5,005, others 17,443—acquired at a high price or by exchange, for relics were then the customary gift from one sovereign to another (just as Sèvres vases are today). He was proud of his collection and had an inventory made of it and asked Cranach to illustrate it with 117 woodcuts and one engraving on copper (the first), which was to be the traditional portrait of the collector and John the Faithful. The work is not brilliant. Cranach alternates careful description (probably embroidered) of the relics with portraits of the saints of whom his master possessed a fragment.

The book came out in 1509 under the title: *Die Zaigung des Hochloswirdigen Heiligtums der Stifft Kirchen aller Heiligen zu Wittemburg*. Cranach's first series of engravings, a *Passio NDJC*, appeared in the same year.

THE ENGRAVINGS

Cranach may have had no knowledge of Dürer's paintings (for we have seen that it was only by visiting the Low Countries that he became aware of the new trends, which he would have seen better in the work of his Nürnberg colleague). But the same cannot be said of the engravings. Some of Cranach's plates are directly descended from Dürer—the *Penance of St. John Chrysostom*, for instance—yet his engravings as a whole are incontestably original. Cranach's lack of recognition today may be due to the present popularity of color reproductions and to the lack of public interest in engravings. After studying the books dealing with his paintings the reader is bound to find some of his work poor and his evolution disconcerting: he is unwilling, therefore, to pay homage to such an uneven and yet surprising artist. But it could be shown that Cranach's was the development of a genius faithful to one individual style, merely by publishing the fourteen woodcuts of his *Passion* and by reproducing the earlier plates such as *St. Chrysostom*, *Original Sin*, the great *Tournaments*, the *Judgment of Paris*, the *Sacrifice of Marcus Curtius*, the *Martyrdom of St. Erasmus*, the *Assumption of Mary Magdalen*, the *St. George*, the *Archangel Michael*, and the *Ascension*, right back to the first Crucifixions.

The scrupulous Passavant doubts whether Cranach made his own woodcuts and engravings on copper: this doubt may stand with regard to the engravings on copper, of which there are few, but the woodcuts are of such a consistently original character that the engraver concerned would have needed exceptional knowledge of the artist. Why not go so far as to say that it was this unique craftsman who gave to

Cranach's engravings the consistency which is not found in his paintings? Great works of art are fated to be wrested from their authors. It is simpler and truer to say that Cranach made his own engravings, and to recognize in him a master whose genius was in full flower.

The earliest Crucifixions of 1500, as we have seen, were exceptionally full of violence. Cranach adds muscles, elongates bodies, breaks them and distends them: his executioners really mean business. Later on, knowledge moderates violence, for no one would dare to call Cranach merely competent in 1509, when the *Passion* engravings appeared. Here the original fire burns just as fiercely, but it is perfectly controlled: the composition is clearer and the drawing is more precise, presenting a wonderful unity of style. The shapes are shown more by delicate strokes (multiplied by the cut, which hardly leaves any blanks for the eye to rest on) than as a massive whole. The same stroke which opens the dramatic event at the top of the page persists to the end, throughout a thousand detours. The whole thing seems piecemeal and

ADAM. 1528
UFFIZI GALLERY, FLORENCE

chaotic, yet there is definite order in it. The composition shows brilliant touches, such as the recumbent figure in the *Crowning with Thorns* which adds to the overwhelming effect of Christ's suffering, the slanting lances and wide blank space at the top of the plate which double the crushing weight of the Saviour's Cross, and the underground effect produced in the *Entombment* by the falling earth and protruding roots beneath which the body is to be laid. But the chief impression left by these engravings is of teeming life, beside which the great Dürer himself appears a little stiff. This shows the high level of Cranach's plates.

His engravings have another significance: they represent defensive action. When Cranach returned from his mission to the Low Countries, he was preoccupied by the reflection of Italian ease and elegance which he had found there. His paintings show that his position was shaken, but his engravings remained firmly rooted on German soil and he countered Mediterranean temptations by this savage series, in which Hans Multscher's grimacing characters once more come to life.

EVE. 1528
UFFIZI GALLERY, FLORENCE

Moreover he had already experimented in the classic style, with nude warriors crowned with laurels passing under a strange-looking cupola, in the *Sacrifice of Marcus Curtius*. The line explores every morsel of flesh here, and the singular feature of the horseman plunging into the ground is well suited to a German artist. Cranach knew what he was about, therefore, when he turned his back on the wide and balanced Italian settings in order to knit his action more closely and far more forcefully.

Perhaps we shall never know why certain plates dated 1506 already bear the mark of the winged serpent, which he had not yet received from his patron. Historians are still arguing about this. Perhaps he simply added his emblematic beast to his arms two years later. This would hardly matter, if there were not among these engravings a *Venus and Cupid* foreshadowing by three years the famous picture in the Hermitage Museum dated 1509—the earliest of Cranach's female nudes.

CRANACH AND THE FEMALE NUDE

It is well known that female nudes were one of Cranach's favorite subjects, and there is universal comment on the apparent incompatibility (nowadays, though not in his own day) between the career of a Reformation artist and that of a purveyor of compliments. It has also been noted that to begin with he painted merry, buxom girls in all the splendor of their maturity (though not with such generous figures as those of Rubens), while as he grew older he preferred to paint them younger and younger, less and less formed. Perhaps he found in them, disguised under Latin and Greek names such as Aphrodite, Lucretia, or Omphale, his best way of making oblation to the new fashion, for his treatment of nudes differed from that of Dürer or of Baldung Grien. When Dürer made his engraving of Adam and Eve in 1504, developing the theme later in a picture dated 1507, his inspiration was obviously twofold: the first, that of the analyst who studies the rabbit, the rhinoceros, and the insect with the same passionate interest, and the second deriving from the first : he was full of wonder, dazzled by the perfection of creation. Dürer could not bring himself to portray our ancestors as fallen creatures. He painted them still shining with innocence, playing with the apples before the Fall, and it is hard to believe on looking at them that knowledge could ever have caused them to fall. Cranach, on the other hand, saw them not from the anatomical point of view but as lovers, as we can tell from the *Adam and Eve* in the Munich Pinakothek, which was painted between 1507 and 1511, according to the historians. He must have been avenging himself against some woman in his treatment of Eve: she is not just plump, she has no feminine graces. The ravishing Catherine of his Dessau altarpiece, painted at the same period, would be turned into a film star by producers today. There is obviously some vengeance going on: Cranach is taking his revenge as a good Catholic for having been driven out of Paradise through his own fault; nevertheless he cannot resist the pleasure of painting his lost Eve with frizzy curls falling in ringlets over her shoulders as far as her small breasts. Indeed he was fascinated at this period by the effect of hair curling round the face, just as later on he was to delight in hats—the large feathered hats of *Landsknechte* or chevaliers set upon the tiny heads of maidens who were invariably nude and who looked more and more like " little minxes " as time went on.

The *Venus* at Leningrad wears a double-stranded necklace and her long hair falls forward over her breasts and down to the small of her back. The finest possible veil, like water, slides from her arm to her thigh, as if to draw attention to her nudity. What can be the inspiration of the male nude figure outlined against the dark background, where a couplet written in shining letters can be seen *(Pelle cupidineos toto con anime luxus, ne tua possideat pectora ceca Venus)*, and of the folded paper showing Cranach's serpent and initials ? Botticelli springs to mind irresistibly. The *Birth of Venus* was painted about 1485, and we know that the figure of

DVM PVER ALVEOLO FVRATVR MELLA CVPIDO.
FVRANTI DIGITVM SEDVLA PVNXIT APIS.
SIC ETIAM NOBIS BREVIS ET MORITVRA VOLVPTAS
QVAM PETIMVS TRISTI MIXTA DOLORE NOCET

Venus had such a success that Botticelli had a number of copies made by his pupils. Some of them, such as the Venus against a black background (Berlin Museum), escaped Savonarola's bonfires, and this Berlin *Venus* may well have been the one which impressed Cranach so deeply. This is quite a credible explanation, but we should be wary of facile comparisons which simply turn painters into a collection of pupils copying each other as hard as they can right under the master's eye. Moreover there is a good deal to be learned from the contrast between the figures. Botticelli's inspiration came more from the classic marble Venus he had seen in the Medici collection than from any model. He had but to adorn the marble in his own elegant manner, and the classic antique became a Botticelli, just as Modigliani "modiglianized" Negro sculpture. Nevertheless it is only an animated statue. Cranach, on the other hand, adorned his Venus with all his memories and all his amorous longings : the Botticellian Venus is the statue of a goddess whose heart beats all of a sudden, but Cranach's Venus is a woman with misty eyes, remote and alluring, nude and therefore mysterious, whom any man (including Cranach) would have admired, had they chanced to meet her in the soft twilight of the picture.

The ninth year of the 16th century can certainly be considered as important for Cranach, for in it he came to a turning point in his career. He was making his mark in every sphere and the main features of his work had already emerged : nudes and figure compositions, paintings of an edifying nature, portraits (he had just painted one of his admirers, the Nürnberg lawyer Christopher Scheurl), and engravings. All his potential was there, and the conflicts of this crowded year illustrate the contradictions of his whole career, which was a perfect reflection of the conflicts rife in Germany at that time.

Moreover he suffered from his own contradictory nature. To begin with, he was an uneven painter. It is hard to believe that the man who painted such masterpieces as the *Martyrdom of St. Catherine* or the Dessau Altarpiece was also responsible

56   PORTRAIT OF MARTIN LUTHER. 1529
UFFIZI GALLERY, FLORENCE

PORTRAIT OF KATHARINA VON BORA, WIFE OF MARTIN LUTHER. 1529
UFFIZI GALLERY, FLORENCE

for such hasty work as the *Man of Sorrows* or the *Carrying of the Cross*, painted in 1515 and now in the Dresden Museum. Cranach's development as a painter shows more than one variation in the whole conception of his work, apart from its quality. We have seen that he changed key abruptly just as he was about to enter the Elector's service, and that he was deeply influenced by his mission to the Low Countries. There were to be further sudden changes throughout his career, none of them so important as the first however. This came when he was illustrating Maximilian's prayer book, about 1514 or 1515, which brought him face to face with Dürer's wonderful work. Dürer's bold assurance must have impressed Cranach, as we can see from his *Adoration of the Magi* at Naumburg, which is an unusual excursion into monumental painting (in the sense that the picture is architecturally conceived).

These foreign invasions into Cranach's work are surprising and disconcerting. No sooner do we think we have grasped the pattern of his career than it suddenly changes; but we should remember to look at the painting of former days in the light of modern art, not forgetting all those contemporary artists whom we suddenly find in the throes of unexpected crises, such as the expressionist experimenting with abstract painting, and vice versa.

If we look on Cranach as our contemporary, we should note that he was always on the side of those who were not bound to any one form of aesthetics. Dürer clung firmly to his own truth, and he departed from it only to replenish his resources in contact with the ancient soil of Germany. Cranach, on the other hand, was perfectly ready to seek counsel where he thought fit, from Quentin Massys or Albrecht Dürer, no matter whom, when embarking on an ambitious composition and not quite sure of himself.

Yet no one ever succeeded in teaching him how to paint freely, with that ease which goes straight to the point and brings out all its meaning. Cranach soon realized the futility of his detours and returned to portraits, isolated figures, and

58

DVM PVER ALVEOLO FVRATVR MELLA CVPIDO
FVRANTI DIGITVM CVSPIDE HIXIT APIS
SIC ETIAM NOBIS BREVIS ET PERITVRA VOLVPTAS
QVAM PETIMVS TRISTI MIXTA DOLORE NOCET

landscapes where he could arrange his characters as the minia-urists did. He was returning to his own truth. It is astonish-ing that after painting such bold compositions during the early part of the century he should have become paralyzed by orderliness. At first sight Cranach does not give the impres-sion of someone violently opposed to new ideas of aesthetics, with his transitory conversions to one formula or another : yet the result is the same as if he were consciously working throughout against innovations in art and in life.

This does not mean that he was a reactionary, fighting against "abstract art" out of loyalty to "impressionism," but rather that he followed a special road of his own. Although his school had no "theorist" it was none the less *avant-garde.*

The portraits of Holbein the Younger are always greatly admired and there can be no doubt that his tragic *Portrait of Wife and Children* is one of the world's masterpieces. Yet Cranach's portraits, too, except for those official likenesses of Frederick the Wise and John the Faithful which he turned out one after the other for Saxon propaganda, are supreme examples of this form of art. They do not flatter, they are as simple as possible while stopping short of caricature, they are well formed and uniquely expressive. To be more precise, they are not just well formed but significant in every line. The picture of the wedding of Sybil of Cleves, for instance, is a perfect example of exact drawing. Each stroke is carried through, each curve has its counterpart ; the fullest value is given to each element. The calm impression conveyed by this ensemble of high tensions is merely a gloss concealing hidden violence. To study this portrait is to realize what Cranach was aiming at: a highly disciplined form of art whose brilliance should spring from its very simplicity. To the man who painted this picture all else would seem mere geometrics or imagery.

THE PICTURE-MAKER OF THE
REFORMATION

Cranach was to become the picture-maker of the Reformation. He saw nothing degrading in this, for he gave his services willingly, just as artists devote their talents to some good cause today. We should recognize, therefore, that Cranach's work is in two keys: to one belongs his "useful" work, voluntarily undertaken, consisting of propaganda for the Electors and decorations for their festivities and for their palaces, and also a series of religious pictures; the second is that of his nudes and portraits, which are purely human and pictorial. We wonder whether the second will get the better of the first, hoping that the first will not spoil the second: but the truth is that the second validates the first. The present-day attempt to set aside Cranach's religious pictures because of their minor quality and dated interest denies their true value.

Jesus Driving the Money-Changers from the Temple may simply be one subject among many to a religious painter, but in Cranach's case it was a sign that battle was joined. Moreover it is interesting because among the faithful in the Dresden picture (painted about 1510) he shows his wife with a baby in her arms, who is probably little Hans. This would not be enough in itself, however, to convince us of the importance Cranach attached to this picture, if we did not know that the German satirists had been ceaselessly refining on Freidank's words: "The nets with which St. Peter caught fish have never been seen in Rome. The nets of the Romans are used to fish for gold and silver." The worst traders of all were those who sold indulgences: this was a common cause of anger in Germany, in which Cranach was at one with all his friends.

The sale of indulgences was indeed the Achilles' heel of the Church. Yet even had there been no traffic in indulgences, some other scandal would have been exposed on which to focus German fury against Rome—that fury which led to the fantastic sack of Rome by the *Landsknechte* in 1527.

John Frederick the Magnanimous, Elector of Saxony. 1533
Georges Renand Collection, Paris

SYBIL OF CLEVES, WIFE OF JOHN FREDERICK THE MAGNANIMOUS, 1533
GEORGES RENAND COLLECTION, PARIS

Cranach was, therefore, among those who were hoping for the reform of Christianity. Frederick the Wise, for his part, made Wittenberg and its University one of the most brilliant centers in Germany and one of the most stormy. In 1508 Luther held the professorship of liberal arts and ten years later Melanchthon was to be a very young Professor of Greek there. The young students whom he taught soon jumped to the conclusion that reformation was only a polite name for revolution. They did not hesitate to stir up riots against the bourgeoisie, even against Cranach himself, who was by then a very rich citizen and a member of the Council of Wittenberg. Luther was to have great difficulty in getting the students to fight for his ideas alone, just as all the leaders of the day were to find themselves outdistanced by their supporters. It was a period of violence, studded with denunciations, arrests, pillage, and street fights, a tenuous and explosive mixture of acts of faith and deeds of folly. After terrible massacres order was finally restored. The reigning princes had by that time taken over the direction of operations and had achieved religious independence, in the financial as well as in the political sphere. No more papal taxes were to be levied : the fiscal monopoly would be in the hands of the Governments.

Frederick the Wise and his successor John Frederick maneuvered to excellent effect. The game was so tricky that they almost lost and John Frederick was in prison for a time, but in 1552 the tables were turned and they won the day.

In 35 years, therefore, the whole affair was settled. It was really a family feud, in which everyone knew his enemy and was on friendly terms with him. Thus Cranach, Luther's friend and disciple, was at one and the same time painting Luther's portrait and that of his worst enemy, Cardinal Albrecht of Brandenburg, who was, of course, thoroughly " papist " and in favor of the sale of indulgences. Cranach also worked for Duke Henry of Saxony, an ardent Roman Catholic. Albrecht of Brandenburg, who had bought himself the Cardinalate of Mainz as a young man, was one of the genuine Maecenases of the 16th century. Dürer worked for him, and his Court painter was Mathias of Aschaffenburg, known as Grünewald. Grünewald painted him as St. Erasmus, beside St. Maurice the Negro, in the Munich Pinakothek picture (1525?). At the time of the peasants' revolt Grünewald, who was on the side of the rebels, had to leave him to seek a miserable refuge at Halle, in Saxon and Lutheran territory. The presence of this inspired and celebrated refugee, whom Melanchthon made much of, did not hinder Cranach from painting the papist tyrant's portrait, not only then but several times later on, which proves how confused the conflict was. Cranach's portraits of the Cardinal strike a curious note, however. One of them is more in the nature of an interior, a kind of study in perspective. We see the Cardinal as St. Jerome, a small figure in the background, seated reading beneath the hat showing his ecclesiastical rank ; but our attention is distracted by the quantities of other things in the room, while various animals—a placid lion, some pheasants, a little dog, and some partridges—wander about under the tables, near baskets of fruit.

The other, of which there were to be several variations, appears to be almost a caricature of Cranach's early St. Jerome. The figure of Christ is bleeding here also, but the body is outstretched as if about to fly, while the loincloth floats out behind the Cross, above rising ground whose rounded shape suggests the earthly planet itself. The bleeding feet of Christ contrast horribly with the plump beringed hands of the Cardinal, who kneels on an enormous cushion of the same scarlet as his gorgeous robes. This stream of red seems to be fed by the blood flowing from the Cross. The Cardinal looks like a butcher gazing meditatively at his meat. A heavy sky, like that in the 1503 *Crucifixion*, covers half the picture, as if portending the end of the world, lending grandeur to this painting of a fat red man kneeling comfortably in a desert at the feet of a crucified Christ.

What can this picture mean? It seems to have been painted without the model, from an engraving on copper of 1520, in which the craftsman working for Cranach modified a print

made by Dürer the year before. If Cranach had wanted to attack the Cardinal in a painting, we would expect him to have done so more openly and with greater ferocity, for he knew very well how to be violent, as the woodcuts of his *Passion* show ; whereas here the satire is only smuggled in. A variation of the picture (now in Berlin) alters the landscape, scattering it with animals, while a caravan of camels appears in the distance. There can be no doubt of the hatred in these pictures. Expressions of opinion such as these, violently proclaimed or introduced by stealth, form a link between the history of the Reformation and the fine arts ; but Cranach gave more direct testimony than this. We know that, together with a fellow member of the Council, he helped to launch Luther's translation of the New Testament.

We know also that Luther was the godfather of Anna, his eldest daughter, and that the painter was a witness at the monk's marriage to the nun Katharina von Bora (which needed a certain amount of courage : Melanchthon refused to come to the wedding). Cranach's numerous portraits of the reformer, his wife, and his relations can be explained by his friendship for them, but he also wished to testify on behalf of the men who were convulsing the Christian world. One picture is a perfect illustration of the reporter's sense of "news" which Cranach possessed. In 1521 Luther, who could not bear it any longer, left the fortress of Wartburg, where he had been hiding since he was proclaimed a public enemy at Worms, and came to Wittenberg. He no longer wore his monk's habit, but had a layman's beard and mustache and went by the name of Junker Jörg. He stayed at Wittenberg just long enough to discuss the situation with Spalatin and Melanchthon, but it gave Cranach time to paint his portrait. We can imagine him embarking on it with his usual energy, throwing himself into one of those "preparations" of which there are several examples in the Rheims Museum—portraits of men and women dashed off lightheartedly but with extraordinary precision and assurance. They are sketches on tinted paper in which oils, watercolor, and gouache are mingled—mat and glossy,

CHRIST WITH THE CHILDREN. 1538

strong and delicate. Later these different techniques had to be brought into harmony. We can imagine the painter taking up one brush after another, working hard at his canvas, while the man who had been banished and excommunicated, whose throat the Emperor's meanest soldier would cheerfully cut, discusses the pressing problems of the cause with his anxious friends. Cranach had just committed himself publicly to this cause by publishing in the same year, 1521, his *Passional Christi und Antichristi,* with Melanchthon's words. It is a comparison in thirteen stages of the life of Christ and that of Antichrist, in other words the Pope. For instance, one left-hand page shows Christ humbling himself by the washing of feet, while on the opposite page the Pope, seated on a dais and raised still higher by the steps of his throne, holds out his foot for the kneeling kings to kiss. Again, on one page we see Christ driving the money-changers out of the Temple and on the other the Pope signing indulgences wholesale. A counter has been set up where the faithful in a throng are paying out their gold, which a clerk pockets, handing them each a parchment duly sealed in return. No modern tract could denounce a scandal more tellingly or rouse anger more effectively. It was not necessary to be able to read to understand that such a Pope was behaving just like Antichrist. There is a point of contact here between those unlettered times and the " readers " of our own day, who are tired of reading and turn far more readily to pictures. Cranach would have had a great success in advertising today.

Erasmus used to say : " Wherever Lutheranism prevails, the study of the humanities loses ground." It is certainly true that this violent pictorial attack on the Pope was directed against one of the most erudite art patrons of all time—Leo X, who was hoping to finance the building of the new Roman Basilica by selling indulgences on a grand scale . . .

Erasmus' comment was not entirely fair, however. Inasmuch as Luther brought him back to the Scriptures it is true that the reformed Christian read less Greek and Latin, yet this did not prevent Cranach from painting Hercules and Lucretia, Venus

VENUS. 1532
STAEDEL INSTITUTE, FRANKFURT ▷

and Diana, and several versions of the Judgment of Paris. It would be wrong to assume that a lack of interest in the humanities corresponded to a denial of art, for the Reformation had its own art, of which Cranach wanted to be the founder. Sometimes Melanchthon suggested subjects or even made preliminary sketches for him. The activities of the Wittenberg iconoclasts must of course have seemed hateful to the painter, while driving him to find a form of art that would satisfy the most intransigent enemy of Catholic imagery. He did not give up his Madonnas and saints, however, and had no hesitation in reissuing the woodcuts of his *Wittenberg Heiligtumsbuch* of 1509, under the new title *Hortulus animae,* and in undertaking a similar inventory of Catholic relics in the churches of Halle in 1520. This shows how broadminded he was, in the uncompromising early days of official Lutheranism.

Moreover at its outset the painting of the Reformation had no such definite character as the rival painting of the Counter Reformation. It was easy to use art as a means of attacking the Pope, but more difficult to find substitutes for a long-standing Marian tradition, and for saints well established in pictorial roles, without constantly painting the crucified Christ and the scenes of the Passion. The faithful needed less harrowing pictures to refresh them. Themes for these were found in the childhood of Christ (though it was hard to hide His Mother) and in various episodes of His life in Jerusalem, which were uncontroversial: we see Him with the woman taken in adultery or at supper with the Pharisee, or uttering the famous words: " Suffer little children . . . to come unto me."

Since it was necessary to teach, the sermon could be written on the picture itself, in gold letters. Thus on the altarpiece of Duke George the Bearded (1534, Meissen Cathedral, Saxony) we read in Latin, above the man's portrait: " Wives should be subject to their husbands as to God. Husbands should care for their wives as for themselves, wives should wear a respectable and decent garment." And above the woman: " Be one with every human creature." In the same way, underneath the picture *Fall and Redemption,* which tells the story of man's original sin, his exile from Paradise on earth, and the Saviour's Ascension, there are quotations from the Bible in six columns, in beautiful Gothic lettering.

The Old Testament is also used as a source of teaching and of new subjects: the *Fall of Pharaoh, Abraham's Sacrifice, Moses and Aaron, Lot and His Daughters, David and Bathsheba, Samson and Delilah, Judith at Holofernes' Banquet, Judith with the Head of Holofernes,* the same head reappearing in the picture of *Salome Presenting the Head of St. John,* having already figured in that of Adam and Eve before the Fall—an example of the painter's own peculiar humor. The Old Testament, however, lent quite a different tone to Cranach's work, approaching that of his courtly figures, of his pictures of Venus and Diana, and of the Judgment of Paris, and of his nude maidens wearing large masculine hats. The beginning of Lot's orgy (Munich Pinakothek) is an example of this. In the distance Sodom blazes, going up in a score of columns of fire whose flames redden the hills: in front of them stands the figure of Lot's wife, already turned into salt, while Lot leads his daughters along the road. Look at them now in the foreground: one daughter, with her hair in disarray, stands pouring wine into a large goblet which the other girl is offering to her father; he is already flushed, busily baring her shoulder and exploring her bodice. An edifying scene, no doubt, though we have to make an effort to veil our eyes and upbraid the poor drunkard and his brats. The reformers' reputation for austerity is dealt a heavy blow by the love with which the painter has treated that loosened hair, those heavy gold chains lying on the naked flesh of the throat, the embroidered scarlet of the dresses, and the mysterious depths of the leafy thicket where the sin is consummated. It is equally hard to see what particular moral significance Cranach could have attached to women of evil life, or to criminal women at least, such as Judith, Salome, or Delilah. In fact he never failed to paint them with a tenderness that appears suspect to us today. Delilah is charming as she cuts the hair of the great Samson lying asleep with

73

I·N·R·I

74 CRUCIFIXION WITH LONGINUS. 1536
NATIONAL GALLERY OF ART, WASHINGTON, D. C. (KRESS COLLECTION)

his head on her lap, still clutching, like a rattle, the jawbone of an ass; and the warriors creeping up on them through the trees seem no more terrible than country policemen about to surprise a couple red-handed. Salome and Judith are both beautifully dressed, one holding the head of St. John on a charger, the other grasping that of Holofernes by the hair, fastidious, smiling, and impassive, with that quizzical look affected by models posing for photographers today.

When Cranach painted women, what can have inspired him to give them that inevitable air of mysterious coldness, that smile which owes more to cosmetics than to happiness, such rich clothing and such heavy jewels in contrast with their delicate skin? It was as if a mechanism were set in motion, so that the painter had no further need of a model. He knew his subject by heart, from the tip of her toes to the top of her head. The subject was dear to his heart, too, and he took enormous pleasure in the painting of it, treating it as a rite.

This pleasure seems to have been shared by his contemporaries, judging by the number of dedicated maidens they painted, whether saints or sinners, pure young girls or minxes, St. Mary or Venus, Lucretia or Salome, all representing the same feminine divinity. But though Cranach's success drove him to paint copies of his own pictures, it never made him prostitute his particular genius in the painting of nudes. The other painters of nudes of his time, such as Baldung Grien and Burgkmair, look like bunglers beside him. He created a special type of female and knew exactly how to bring out her latent eroticism; and he was so sure of himself and of the effect of his work that he did not trouble greatly over literary, historical, and mythological justification for his nudes, even though Biblical and mythological references were almost essential at that period.

We are not greatly concerned that he had only the slenderest justification for giving the name of Lucretia to those little nudes veiled in gauze, with their tiny breasts and delicate shape, small heads and expressionless faces—nudes that he was so often to repeat, careless as to whether anyone should think that he was thereby endangering their perfection. But in his picture of *Three Young Girls* (in the Vienna Museum) he glories openly in their tender flesh, exquisite jewelry, and fashionable clothes : it is a triple feast of painting. There is something particularly appealing to us today in such beauty, free of moral lessons and of no historical importance. The painter seems here to be entirely single-minded, conscious only of the pleasure of painting. Perhaps this is a portrait of three sisters, or again it may simply represent three of the costumes which Cranach designed for Court ceremonies—no matter, the picture moves us by its beauty alone. There is something unique about it, giving us an insight into the artist's deep nature. He was not only set apart from the other painters of his day by his ever-growing search for a pictorial style of his own, amounting almost to a calligraphy, perfect in grace and reserved in expression; he *was* apart, living his own secret life. Cranach, the militant Reformer, courtier, statesman, and merchant, was at heart a solitary. Where could so public a painter take refuge ? When we think of his " expressionist " beginnings we realize at what high cost he achieved his secrecy.

He was so overwhelmed with commissions that it is easy to see why he became secretive, learning to express himself un- obtrusively both for his own sake and in self-defense. It is an accepted fact that Cranach was the richest citizen and land- owner in Wittenberg. In 1528 he paid 4,066 guilders in taxes, which shows how successful he had become. He was a regular member of the Council and was three times elected Burgo- master. He married off his daughters well (with dowries), and in 1878 the Wittenberg pharmacy which he had founded was still in the hands of his descendants. He had accumulated a substantial fortune. In 1520 the Elector gave him a monopoly as apothecary : " Except at fair times, no one except Lucas, whether resident or stranger, may trade in spices, preserves, theriaca, colored wax, or any other commodity which apothe- caries usually sell." This monopoly gave rise to scandal. It was said that his products were bad, that he did not supervise his

dispensary properly because he was so busy with his other trades of printing, publishing, and painting, and complaint was laid in the appropriate quarter, so that Frederick was obliged to decree : " Since Lucas does not carry out his apothecary's business efficiently, since he deals in other trades, and leaves his pharmacy in the hands of servants, the said Lucas shall be subject to the military obligations incumbent upon all the citizens of Wittenberg ! "

He was a bourgeois and a wealthy citizen ; and he did very good business. His fame was such that calls were made on him from all sides. The ruling family of Saxony required the services of the Elector's Court painter—George the Bearded as much as Henry the Pious—not only for portraits but for altar-pieces and allegories, to decorate palaces and organs, paint ceilings, design festive costumes and choose color schemes for suites of rooms, for the urgent manufacture of two thousand shields to be borne into battle by a Hesso-Saxon coalition army, for the engraving by the thousand of portraits of the Elector who had just died or of the Elector who had just married, to design his tomb, to contrive portraits of his an-cestors which he could hang in his room, and to decorate the courtroom of the Town Hall with appropriate figures. A Prussian gentleman orders books, a Cardinal of Mainz a picture of the Holy Family, and Frederick, having one day seen Dürer's *Apocalypse,* desires his Court painter to make one for him. Add to all this the requirements of Lutherans in a hurry to bring out some vital book or pamphlet for immediate distribution and in need of paintings or engravings of Luther and his wife, of Melanchthon or Spalatin, and it is easy to see that Cranach's life was that of a factotum.

He managed nevertheless to follow an important political career (for to be Burgomaster of Wittenberg, the scene of endless disturbances, can have been no sinecure), to achieve his own personal ambitions as a painter, and to die at a respectable old age, his fortune made.

Cranach's studio was able to satisfy all the demands upon it, for the artist of those days was a kind of contractor to whom one applied for his particular style of work, its quality being guaranteed by his reputation. His studio and its colossal output tell against Cranach today : if he had not produced so much perhaps he would be better appreciated. It is certainly very necessary to differentiate carefully between his own original work and that of his studio, so that all that is of real quality can be attributed to him and much that is mediocre to his studio.

There are several pointers to guide us : first of all the serpent with lowered wings, the personal mark of Lucas the Younger, which at once helps us to differentiate. On the other hand, the studio's work does not usually bear the family mark. There can be no doubt that the studio was responsible for such simple tasks as the copies of Dürer's engravings, the *Portrait of Cardinal Albrecht of Brandenburg* (1520), or the simplified replicas of the *Apocalypse* surrounding six original plates. The engraving of the arms which each family wished to own was also done by the studio, as well as the paintings and engravings of the princes of Saxony distributed by their propaganda machine to the four corners of Europe, to their allies, vassals, and friends.

It is astounding that Cranach himself should not have been completely absorbed in the direction and management of this factory. As for his sons, we do not know when Hans, the elder, was born; we only know that he died at Bologna in 1537. Flechsig attributes an important picture to him, and he is supposed to have been the pseudo-Grünewald who worked for the Cardinal of Mainz, Albrecht of Brandenburg. However this may be, it is strange that the elder son did not enter his father's business. His age and right of seniority made him the appointed heir, and we have no grounds at all for supposing that aesthetic or religious differences estranged him from his father. It is probable that he went to Bologna to study geometry and perspective. Albrecht Dürer had been initiated into this form of art, and he praised it highly.

The life and work of the younger son are better known. Lucas the Younger was born in 1515. His mark appeared in 1537, that is to say when the news of his brother's death put an end to any hope that Hans would join in the family's work. Lucas married twice : in 1541 Barbara Bruck, in 1551 a Fräulein Schurff, both of good Lutheran families. His style resembles that of his father, though the drawing is perhaps less close and less nervous. Lucas painted and engraved portraits of the ruling family of Saxony. He worked with his father and it was he who completed the great altarpiece in the Church at Weimar, the last picture Lucas the Elder undertook : the *Allegory of the Redemption.* In general his paintings, with the exception of his portraits, try to express too much. Nothing is left in the dark, as if meticulous theologians were supervising his art. Each detail is perfect, yet the whole effect is confused. Lucas the Younger inherited his father's faults, but not those flashes of originality which place Lucas the Elder among the great masters. The son's originality is merely bizarre. There are two large pictures by him in the Dresden Museum of an episode in the life of Hercules. One shows the giant asleep, with the pygmies about to capture him ; in the other he is awake, chasing his tiny enemies. The humor is so heavy that we are not amused. Cranach the Elder going back to prehistory to tell the story of a scuffle between bearded and beardless men is a good deal more humorous. Cranach the Younger was never more than an honest craftsman from a provincial studio. Moreover, after Luther's death in 1546 and the Protestant victory six years later Wittenberg ceased to be the revolutionary center of Christianity, becoming merely a small town which pilgrims visited to see the " Luther Halle."

In 1541, Cranach the Elder's wife died. He had married off his son Lucas shortly before that, and he next married off two of his daughters, in 1543 and 1544. Although now in his seventies, he was as active as ever. John Frederick the Magnanimous, husband of the remarkable Sybil of Cleves, had not the bonhomie of Frederick the Wise. A pronounced squint gave him a crooked look, aggravated by his air of arrogance. He was determined to outdo his predecessors in magnificence, however, and his Court painter had more work than ever. He also encouraged Cranach in his Protestant religious painting, for he was even more in favor of the Reformation than Frederick and at the first opportunity, in 1526, he proclaimed Lutheranism as the official religion. Of course this gave him the chance of seizing the monks' possessions, but its most important result was to bring order into a country where new sects were being formed every day and where there was a crying need for a simple regime with no more disputes, after the terrible wars between the knights and the peasants. Luther and Melanchthon set to work all over the country, organizing parishes, spreading the new liturgy, and making sure of the pastors' loyalty, and the painters were called upon to provide pious pictures for the churches.

We have seen how devotedly Cranach worked to lay the foundation of Protestant painting: one of the most characteristic examples is the altarpiece in Wittenberg Cathedral, depicting the Lord's vineyard. Part of the vineyard is being plundered by the Roman clergy, while the remainder is being cultivated by the heroes of the Reform. The whole picture is obviously a late work, for which he may only have given directions. We may well wonder what happened to Cranach the Elder's genius when the serpent lowered its wings. He was so busy directing his studio, supervising his shops, and governing his town that he effaced himself behind paintings devoted to spreading the word of God, until he was nothing more than a pictorial fighter for the Reformation. He was no longer Cranach the painter. He was the picture-maker of the Reformation.

Poring over dates and pictures, we seek desperately for the master who painted the *Portrait of Sybil of Cleves,* the *Three Young Girls* of Vienna, *Lot's Daughters,* the pictures of Venus and of the Judgment of Paris, the portraits of Henry the Pious and of Luther's family. Cranach's biographers tell us that in 1550, according to the archives, he was still painting portraits and mythological scenes for his imprisoned master, John Frederick the Magnanimous. According to tradition he met Titian at Augsburg in this same year and drew his portrait, but what remains of all this? The painter gradually disappears behind a façade of intense activity, but in 1537, when his elder son died and he passed his arms to his younger son, Cranach's genius was nearing exhaustion. There was proof of its periodical revival or resurrection in the great *Fountain of Youth* (1546), which was in the Berlin Museum and was destroyed during the last war. After that date, however, there were only Protestant pictures, regarding which we are perfectly willing to praise the militant's devotion to his cause but seek the great painter's work in vain, ascribing their dullness to Lucas the Younger.

Cranach was to be remembered after his death as a victorious and loyal fighter. War broke out in 1546. The troops of Saxony, Hesse, and Württemberg, of the Elector Palatine, of Augsburg, Strasbourg, Ulm, and Constance fought against the infantry of Charles V, whom Maurice of Saxony supported, determined to take John Frederick's place as Elector. Finally the Emperor cornered John Frederick in the city of Muhlberg and took him prisoner, wounded, on April 24, 1547. Cranach was at his side. He learned that the Emperor's Spanish soldiers had destroyed the paintings he had made in the Chapel of Torgau Castle, and his one thought was to protect from pillage the altarpieces and works of art in Wittenberg, hoping to arrange for their transport to the Low Countries (there was a Dürer among them, *The Martyrdom of the Ten Thousand,* which he particularly wanted to save). He sought out Charles V, therefore, whom he had known as a child, reminding him that he had painted his portrait in 1508, at the time of his mission to the Low Countries, and begging him to mitigate his master's captivity and to put an end to the war against the Lutherans. A new

Elector was installed at Wittenberg. Maurice of Saxony came into power, and might well have thought himself firmly established in a pacified country. He proceeded to issue the usual decrees. Far from being angry with Cranach for his loyalty to the enemy, he renewed his monopoly as apothecary, hoping thus to make him desert John Frederick. Cranach's son-in-law also begged him to leave the prisons where he shut himself up voluntarily. John Frederick, for his part, was short of money and could no longer pay his Court painter. It was all to no avail: Lucas the Elder followed his master, whom the Emperor dragged after him from Weimar to Augsburg (where Cranach's meeting with Titian took place) and thence to Innsbruck. There the story gains momentum. Maurice of Saxony changed sides and suddenly attacked the Emperor, forcing him to leave Innsbruck with his meager escort. Charles V dragged John Frederick (and possibly Cranach too) on a fantastic escapade across the Brenner Pass at night in a snowstorm. It was the only way of escape. What that night must have meant to Cranach, aged 80, can well be imagined. The hour of Charles V's surrender to Lutheranism had struck, however, and the Protestant princes were henceforth to be masters of their own countries—in religious matters as in all else. The Treaty of Passau (1552) restored John Frederick to his rights after five years of captivity, and Cranach made a triumphal return to Saxony.

He had one more year to live as a national hero. He helped to begin the altarpiece, gigantic for Germany (approximately 20 feet long and 10 feet high), which was to commemorate him forever as one of the reformers of Christianity. Perhaps he made the sketch for this picture celebrating restoration and victory—victory first of all, for Cranach and Luther are shown in the center panel, while John Frederick the Magnanimous and his family are relegated to the side panels.

Lucas Cranach the Elder died on October 16, 1553, and was buried in the cemetery of St. James at Weimar. He is described on his tombstone as a "most excellent painter."

Perhaps he would rather have been praised for some other quality than that of his speed as a painter.

If Cranach came to Paradise, in which Eden would his lot fall? Perhaps in the Lord's vineyard, in that part of it so well raked and well tended by the same heroes of the Reformation whom Cranach painted for the good cause; or in that large park of his, full of trees loaded with fruit, and of flowers, where does, stags, and pheasants roam and where big white greyhounds sleep, those animals whom Dürer in his *Melencolia* raised to the status of symbols but who are here simply beasts at peace, like the swans floating on the calm waters. This is the Eden we would wish for him. He may have fought for the former, but as we look at his paintings we know that it is in the latter that he would be happy. Here he led his Venus, here his stags were hunted. It is a wide landscape, half wild, half cultivated, where the rivers flow gently, where the hills provide grottoes and the thickets arbors for those secret assignations he loved to have with his charming Eve; the bearded God who beholds them and drives them forth does not really seem to take their sins seriously, only punishing them with a father's tenderness. Yes, indeed, let us wish for him such a Paradise, presided over by an amiable deism, where the ancient legends seem more amusing than frightening and where all is rather vague.

For it cannot be denied that Cranach proved his genius in profane rather than in sacred art, even though toward the end of his days he seemed to deny the original sin of his sensual Court style, as it must have appeared to a militant Lutheran. Sacred and profane did not keep pace for long. The first gradually killed the second; but it has ill survived.

His was a strange career and a strange life. There was a complete break in his style when he was 31. His output was amazing even when he was past 60. His greatest achievements were masterpieces of ease and talent, bearing witness to his complete originality. Next must rank his devout, public-spirited, and courageous life, and his old age as a national hero, with its apotheosis on the walls of the Cathedral.

LIST OF ILLUSTRATIONS